STRATEGIC THINKING

sound
wisdom
Because Your Success Matters

SOUND WISDOM BOOKS
BY EARL NIGHTINGALE

Lead the Field

The Direct Line

The Strangest Secret

Successful Living in a Changing World

Your Success Starts Here: Purpose and Personal Initiative

Transformational Living: Positivity, Mindset, and Persistence

Your Greatest Asset: Creative Vision and Empowered Communication

Master Your Inner World: Overcome Negative Emotions, Embrace Happiness, and Maximize Your Potential

THE STRANGEST SECRET SERIES

30 Days to Self-Confidence: A Guide to Stop Doubting Yourself and Start Succeeding

The Power of Goals: Timeless Lessons on Finding Purpose, Overcoming Doubt, and Taking Action

Habits for Success: The Pathway to Self-Mastery & Freedom

The Secret Advantage: Proven Principles for Financial Success

Strategic Thinking: Improve Mental Clarity, Solve Problems, Become More Creative

EARL NIGHTINGALE

STRATEGIC THINKING

Improve Mental Clarity, Solve Problems, and Become More Creative

THE STRANGEST SECRET SERIES

Published and distributed by:
SOUND WISDOM
P.O. Box 310
Shippensburg, PA 17257-0310
717-530-2122

info@soundwisdom.com

www.soundwisdom.com

ISBN 13 TP: 978-1-6409-5505-9

ISBN 13 eBook: 978-1-6409-5506-6

For Worldwide Distribution, Printed in the U.S.A.

1 2 3 4 5 6 7 8 / 29 28 27 26 25

Your world is a living expression of how you have used your mind.

—EARL NIGHTINGALE

CONTENTS

INTRODUCTION

by Vic Conant

My dad, Lloyd Conant, met Earl Nightingale in 1956 when Earl was a popular radio commentator on WGN in Chicago. At the time, Dad was a successful business-man, he owned his own direct marketing and printing company. Earl had just produced a recording titled *The Strangest Secret* and was looking for someone to market that product. The two of them met and Dad ended up selling a million of that recording over the years. These two men were a match made in Heaven. My dad the marketer and Earl the talent.

Earl, like Lloyd, was a "Great Depression" era child and grew up poor in California. Earl educated himself; he was an avid reader and a brilliant guy. Both had only a high school education. Earl was a totally self-made man as was my dad, so the two of them hit it off and eventually created Nightingale-Conant when I was about 14.

Every individual who has discovered what Earl Nightingale calls *The Strangest Secret* throughout the ages has found it to be a profoundly life-changing discovery. That secret? *You become what you think about*—and the fact that our thoughts *control* and many believe *create* our reality. Consequently, there is great responsibility placed on our thinking, making us responsible for our own future.

Vic Conant
Chairman of the Board
Nightingale-Conant Corporation

Note: As Earl's wisdom was shared with audiences worldwide in the 1950s and 1960s, some statistics and other pertinent information have been updated as footnotes revealing the gravity of his teachings then—and how impactful and relevant they still are today.

1

THINKING CLEARLY

What thinking skills are you using to become a more strategic thinker?

The Power of Thought

Here's a good question for you and it's a vital one: *As far as your life and future are concerned, what do you think about most of the time?* You tell any expert what it is you think about most of the time, and he can tell you what kind of a person you are and what your future very probably will be like.

There's always been a lot of mystery and fraud and hocus pocus surrounding fortune-tellers, and there ought to be. But if you spend an hour just talking to an intelligent and discerning person, that person can tell you a great deal about yourself and your future. Ralph Waldo Emerson wrote, "A man is what he thinks about all day long." It's really as simple as that. You are literally what you think about. By analyzing your thoughts, you can analyze yourself.

Just as the alcoholic thinks about alcohol, the dope addict about dope, the criminal about crime, the medical student thinks about medicine, the lawyer about law, the young mother about her children and her husband. We are, as Emerson wrote, what we think about all day long.

Of course during the course of a day, we think about many things, hundreds of things—but what controls our lives is what we think about most of the time. So if you can tell me or anybody what you think about most of the time, I or anybody else can tell you what you are. Knowing this gives people who understand this fact, a really remarkable measure of control over their lives. Since

By analyzing your thoughts, you can analyze yourself.

we become what we think about, and since we can control our thinking, we can to an altogether unsuspected extent, control our life and future.

As one of the world's greatest psychologists put it, "If you only care enough for a result, you will almost certainly attain it. If you wish to be rich, you'll be rich. If you wish to be learned, you'll be learned. If you wish to be good, you'll be good. Only you must then really wish these things and wish them exclusively and not wish at the same time, a hundred other incompatible things just as strongly."

Confusion Thinking Versus Decision Thinking

In my opinion, confusion in people's lives can be traced to confusion in their thinking. On the other hand, people who know what they want and have decided to reach their goals at all costs, are for the most part, happy and well-directed people who will achieve their goals goes.

So it all comes down to this then, deciding on what it is you want more than anything else is the most important decision you can make. Once you make this decision, keep to it. Think about it all day long, stay everlastingly at it. And then instead of being on a river that winds all over the countryside, you'll find yourself on a straight road, the shortest distance between where you are now and the point where you want to arrive. So remember the words of Ralph Waldo Emerson, "A man..." and this goes for a woman too, "is what he thinks about all day long."

Now, what are you thinking about right at this moment?

There's some debate on whether thinking skills can be taught. It is agreed that thinking skills are learned. We're born with thinking skills. Thinking skills are one of the most important components of competency. What works at a given situation may not work at all and another even slightly different situation.

For our purposes here, let's address two areas of thinking. *Critical thinking* is focused on deciding what to believe or do, and *creative thinking* is the ability to come up with new combinations of ideas to fulfill a need.

On the topic of teaching thinking skills, education basics focus on *remembering* as opposed to *thinking*. Learning to think instead of just memorizing requires basics such as gathering facts through research and experience, thoughts directed at skills you can actually do and not just only think you can do. That requires some organizational structure to build competence. Earl spoke of what an education can do for you and the structure to get the most from it.

Education Versus Knowledge

Mention the word "education," and most think of knowledge. There was an influential and controversial woman named Annie Besant. She was proud of her heritage and supported the cause of Irish self-rule throughout her adult life. Self-rule or autonomy describes the competence to exercise all of the necessary functions of power without intervention from any kind of authority.

Annie Besant, born in 1847 and died in 1933 was a very busy, interesting, and hardworking woman. She wrote a great many things, founded colleges, spent a great many years in India working to improve conditions and so on. She was an extremely controversial woman, but she carved a place in history for herself and her heart was definitely in the right place.

She lived 86 busy years, but she wrote something once, just a short little thing that I like very much, and I'd like you to read it. She wrote, "Knowledge is essential to conquest, only according to our ignorance are we helpless. Thought creates character. Character can dominate conditions, will creates circumstances and environment." I think you'll agree that Annie could put a great deal into a very few words. You could take that quotation and write ten volumes about it.

Let's look at this quote a little bit at a time. She wrote, *"Knowledge is essential to conquest, only according to our ignorance are we helpless,"* and that's the first sentence. A conquest covers many things, all things. It could be anything from passing to the next highest grade in school, getting that new car you have your eye on, marrying the person you picked out, or whatever the

"Knowledge is essential to conquest, only according to our ignorance are we helpless. Thought creates character. Character can dominate conditions, will creates circumstances and environment."

problem you're interested in conquering. It takes knowledge to do it.

So you could pose that sentence another way, "The more knowledge a person has, the more things he or she can achieve." Makes sense, doesn't it? So all a person has to do is decide what it is he or she wants and then start getting the knowledge needed to get it.

"Only according to our ignorance are we helpless. Thought creates character." Character is defined as the aggregate of qualities that distinguishes one person or thing from others.

We might say that the more qualities a person has, the more character the person has. "Thought creates character," well then the more we think, the more character we create. So mental clarity thinking becomes pretty important because she goes on to say that character can dominate conditions. In other words, if we don't like the conditions in which we find ourselves or at least want to improve our condition, we can do it by developing more character or by thinking more about ourselves and our place in the world.

Being able to dominate conditions is a way of telling our own fortune, isn't it? And we'd all like to do that, at least to the degree that we're able as mortals to do it.

So character becomes vital to us, and the quotation ends with the words, *"Will creates circumstances and environment."* That could be put another way by saying we will

If we don't like
the conditions
in which we find
ourselves or at
least want to
improve our
condition, we
can develop more
character by
thinking more
about ourselves
and our place
in the world.

become as far as our circumstances and environment are concerned what we will. And this is another way of saying our environment is a reflection of our minds. So what kind of circumstances and environment do you want? You can control it in better than 99 percent of the cases.

Lack-of-Knowledge Consequences

All across the country, the world for that matter, there are literally millions and millions of human beings who live in an almost constant state of confusion and unhappiness. And you know why? I believe it's because they're either conceited or ignorant or both.

Let me explain.

Just about all great men and women in the past and in the present have told us how they have achieved the kind of life they wanted to live, how they have come to be successful and lead rewarding lives. It's all been written thousands of times.

The great prophets have told us, the great philosophers have told us—Descartes, Spinoza, Leibniz, Schopenhauer, Hegel, Emerson, James, they're almost countless. Our own modern business leaders and educators have told us of their philosophies that have guided them to the lives they wanted to live and lead.

Throughout the ages, men and women have died by the thousands so that these great living truths could be passed along to you and me and our youngsters—so we can learn from our betters, from those who have gone before, and those who have achieved what we would like to achieve or at least partly achieve during our own lifetimes.

If people are not getting to where they want to be, if they are confused and in an almost constant state of bitterness or cynicism, it's either because they are conceited or ignorant or both. If they know about the tons of literature written on this subject and don't believe it, they are conceited. They think they are smarter than all the great prophets, the brilliant philosophers who ever lived.

We can learn from our betters—those who have achieved what we would like to achieve.

If they don't know this material exists, they are ignorant, but at least there's still hope for them once they get their hands on it.

So unless you're living the kind of life you want to live, it's either because you don't believe what you've learned or you haven't learned what you need to know. In either case, if you've been an adult for any length of time, it's your fault. Nobody is going to come and take us by the hand and lead us to knowledge.

If we haven't enough sense to dig it out for ourselves, well, we're just going to have to suffer the consequences. I'm sure we all pity the beggar who comes up to us asking for money he has not earned in the midst of a busy modern city. But we don't pity him because his clothes are filthy or because he has no money, we pity him because he lacks the only thing on earth that could help him— information, knowledge. It's the lack of this that makes us poor, that makes beggars of us.

This lack is what makes us live lives of meanness and frustration in an abundant world—conceit or ignorance, we must choose which of these words best describes us if we're not living or on the road to the life we seek. No man or woman on earth has the right to be conceited, because when a person is conceited, that individual isn't important.

There's nothing wrong with being ignorant when we're young, but there is no one more deserving of pity than the person who remains ignorant and who keeps the windows and doors closed to the light of truth and freedom.

Ralph Perry wrote, "Ignorance deprives men of freedom because they do not know what alternatives there are. It's impossible to choose to do what one has never heard of." And Confucius said, "Ignorance is the night of the mind, but a night without moon or star."

One time I read a book written by a psychologist about a man who said to him, "Doctor, I'd give anything if I'd gone to college."

So the doctor asked, "Well, why don't you go?"

And the man answered, "Well, because I'm thirty-five years old, married, have two children, and it would take me ten years to go through college at night."

What excuses are there for not gaining knowledge and becoming a great thinker?

So the doctor asked, "Well, tell me how old will you be in ten years if you go to college?"

The man replied, "Why, I'll be forty-five."

The doctor asked, "How old would you be in ten years if you don't go to college?"

The man thought a moment and said slowly, "Forty-five, I guess," and was completely confused that the age came out to be the same.

Time passes anyway. And if we want something very much, the passing of the years will not change our wanting it, but may only deepen our frustration and feelings of inadequacy. Now, I'm not saying everyone should go to college. Far from it. I don't think everyone should. What I am saying is that if there's something you wish you had accomplished but didn't, and if it's good, look at it logically, can you still do it?

I read recently about a woman who graduated from college out West and she was in her sixties. If there's something you want very much to do, whatever it may be, and if it's good, why not do it? If you want to do it badly enough, the chances are you can find a way.

World of Words

The power of thought—of mental clarity—is a critical issue to becoming confident and using the power of a positive attitude to achieve your goals, aspirations, dreams.

We live in a world of words. No matter what something happens to be, we have a word for it and some words mean a great deal to us. Words such as love, happiness, success, achievement, joy, ability. These words describe conditions all of us want, but there's one word that controls them all that is. There's one word that describes a condition that will bring us all of these things, or keep us from getting any one of them. It's been called the most important word on earth.

And if from all the many thousands of words in the language, you are asked to select the one that would influence your life more than any other, could you pick the right word? I've talked about it before in my books and recordings. In our language, it's pronounced *attitude*. Once we're grown and on our own, this word actually controls our environment, our entire world.

If your attitude toward the world is good, you'll obtain good results. If your attitude is excellent, you'll obtain excellent results. If your attitude is bad, you'll obtain bad results, and if your attitude is just so-so, you live in a world that's not particularly bad or particularly good, just so-so.

If you're curious about what kind of an attitude you have, a simple test will tell you what your attitude has been up to this point in your life. Just answer this question with a yes or no: Do you feel the world is treating you well? If your answer is a quick yes, your attitude is good. If your answer is no, your attitude is bad. And if you have trouble deciding, your attitude is probably average. You see, our environment, which is another way of saying how the world treats us, is nothing more than a reflection, a mirror actually of our own attitude.

One of the most pitiful aspects of society is the really large percentage of people who lead dismal, narrow, darkened lives, crying out against what appears to be a cruel world, which they believe has singled them out for an existence of trouble, misery, and bad luck. Anyone who finds themselves in such a prison of discontent should face the fact that they have very probably built a prison with their own hands. And unless a person changes, the cell will continue to grow smaller and darker.

The world doesn't care whether we change or not. Adopting a good healthy attitude and healthy mental outlook toward life will positively affect us and the people surrounding us.

As it says in the Bible, as you sow, so shall you reap. It would be impossible to even estimate the number of jobs that have been lost, the number of promotions missed, the number of sales not made, and the number of marriages ruined by having a poor attitude. Yet you can number in the millions, the jobs that are held but hated, the marriages that are tolerated, but unhappy, all because of people who are waiting for others or the world to change toward them—instead of being big

Anyone finding themselves in a prison of discontent should realize that they have probably built that prison with their own hands.

enough and wise enough to realize that we get back only what we put out.

Amazing Life-Changing
Thirty-Day Test

In 30 days you can change your world and your environment by making a simple test for 30 days. The test? *Treat every person you meet, without any exceptions, as the most important person on earth.* You'll find that they will begin treating you the same way.

Wrote Viktor E. Frankl in *Man's Search for Meaning*, "Everything can be taken from a man but one thing: the last of the human freedoms—to choose one's attitude in any given set of circumstances, to choose one's own way." Attitude being an inner aspect that can keep us free, even fairly cheerful regardless of the environment in which circumstances may have placed us. The ancient philosophers had discovered this fact, but it seems that each maturing person must rediscover it for ourselves to define our own brand of freedom—by thinking clearly.

Good Dr. Viktor E. Frankel, psychiatrist and Holocaust survivor, also wrote, "Fear makes come true that which one is afraid of." Even if it only comes true in the imagination, we must experience the tortures of what we fear, tortures often as worse as those if what we feared actually came to pass physically in our lives. It's why the old line, "A coward dies a thousand deaths, a brave man dies but once" is really true.

Innovative Thinking

Innovation drives positive changes in efficiency, productivity, quality, competitiveness, and market share. Peter Drucker, the famous management consultant, was a leader in the development of management education. He invented the concept known as management by

When it comes to innovation, the importance of ideas should not be underestimated.

objectives and self-control. He's been described as the founder of modern management and wrote that *Innovation is the specific function of entrepreneurship, whether in an existing business, a public service, institution, or a new venture started by a loan individual in the family kitchen.* Mental clarity is the means by which the entrepreneur either creates new wealth producing resources or endows existing resources with enhanced potential for creating wealth. When it comes to innovation, the importance of ideas should not be underestimated.

Ideas are the most important things on earth, and each of us has our own idea factory. It comes as standard equipment at birth, the big brain of the homo sapiens, the single surviving member of the genus homo. The baby is born and we hold in our hands a miraculous living creature whose potential is unknown. What will enter that astonishing brain? And from those ingredients, what kind of life will this child fashion?

It's too bad that *thinking* is not a required course in the public schools. Not *remembering,* which is what most schoolwork is about. Rather, *thinking* 1, 2, 3, 4, and so on, right into the higher realms of university education. Mental clarity thinking is the highest function of which the human being is capable—yet it is not taught in our nation's schools. Thinking is taken for granted.

What every working person should receive upon finishing a training program offered by his employer is a tape program. The program might be called Your Life and Your

Work. In it would be found much of the material we're dealing with here, plus such lessons as recommended savings plans, emergency planning, and simple aptitude tests designed to help find the main area of a person's inherent competence.

There is a book titled *Know Your Own Mind* by James Greene and David Lewis.[1] This book contains nine tests that tell readers what they do best. As it says on the back cover:

> In it you will learn from only nine quick and easy to do exercises...

- What kind of thinking—inductive, deductive, et cetera you do easily—and how you could use this skill to enrich and reroute your life.

- How to determine your degree of creativity— and maximize it to bring more useful ideas into your life.

- How to assess your ability to interact with others. And how to broaden those skills to reach more people.

- How to determine what's easiest for you to learn.

---

1. Ross and Associates, New York.

How to turn what you find out about yourself in this speedy book to best advantage in your personal life and career—where you'll be happiest and what you'll do best and much more.

The thing is, all of this stuff is fascinating to the person and opens up all sorts of interesting windows of opportunity. Options, options, options. The very things we need if we're to make the kinds of plans that will maximize at least to some degree what we are and what we can do. And this program would have a section headed, you have lost your job and the section would deal with the subject what can you do that the community wants or needs? The community being the entire United States and the free world.

After the initial shock and period of depression, we often find ourselves in work much more to our liking and with far more opportunity for advancement than ever afforded by the old job. Surveys of men and women of singular success have shown that their success hinged directly on the jobs they had left behind. Whether they'd quit voluntarily or been fired made no difference.

Practically, all of the top people in our corporation were formally employed by other companies. That they're delighted with their present work proves my point. They find their work far more interesting and earning more in the way of rewards than ever before in their lives.

There's an excellent theory in business—we should not concentrate our thinking on the things that are going badly or in need of change, but rather on those things that are going best and producing the most revenue. That's where our thinking can have the greatest return.

To act on an idea, note that innovations require only three things: 1) find a need and fill it; 2) competent people are needed to succeed with relevant technology; 3) financial support. For now, let's focus on the core dynamic of competency. Strategic thinking people continue improving throughout life.

Needed: Competent People

The human drive to work and participate in society is most interesting to observe. The other morning I watched two cooks at work. It was 10 o'clock on a Sunday morning at Denny's restaurant in Monterey, California. The place was packed. Breakfast orders festooned the order wheel and completed breakfasts were lined up on the hot counter awaiting their proper servers.

The cooks worked fast and efficiently. Their concentration absolute as they served up hot pancakes, eggs, bacon, sausages, ham, toast, English muffins, biscuits. No one could work faster with such efficiency. No two orders were exactly the same eggs, sunny side up, over easy, scramble, lightly basted, over well. It was tiring to watch them, yet they were completely absorbed at their peak and enjoying the experience. Watching them, I realized once again how important our work is to our well-being and how important doing our work well is to our well-being.

Our job is much, much more than a means of making a living. It establishes our identity and awards quality and meaning to our lives. It makes our leisure time free from anxiety and allows us to look at people in the world squarely in the eyes. We belong. We earn our keep. Without work, we're crippled, truncated beings.

I have obtained ten times more education since leaving school than what I obtained while a student. I can go at my own pace, choose my own subjects—and you can do the same. If your goal involves a degree or degrees in subjects that cannot be learned at home, but demand residency at a college or university, you can do that too.

For example, if your goal is sufficiently important to you, it's difficult to learn brain surgery at home or advanced biology or chemistry. For many subjects, school attendance is required; but realize that the years will continue to pass, whether you prepare for your compelling goal or not.

So why not go to work on it? Our education should end only when we do—and the process of education can be endlessly fascinating. We're never without something interesting to do. New books to order and read, new projects to undertake. We can become teachers if we

Our education should end only when we do—and the process of education can be endlessly fascinating.

like and pass our enthusiasm and skills on others similarly inclined.

Keep studying your specialty. Go to meetings and conventions on the subject if you feel they'll help. Soak up all you can, participate in any way you can, become involved, but leave plenty of time to work toward your goal. Don't become so bogged down in various service activities that you don't have time—the important core time to devote to your journey.

I recall many years ago I was invited to join a writer's club. The club met once a week for lunch, at which time various writers were discussed or appeared to give a talk. I made such a talk myself. After having been a member for a few weeks, I told them the club was apparently for people who wanted to talk about wanting to be a writer, so I dropped out.

I was a real writer. I wrote for a living. The people in the so-called Writers Club were dilettantes, not writers. They wanted to talk like writers, talk about writing and rub shoulders with writers, but the mornings did not find the seat of their pants sitting in front of the typewriter. They wrote in quotation marks for their own amusement when the mood struck. Perhaps it's well that they wrote for their own amusement because I don't think anyone was about to pay for what they wrote. They should have taken under Hemingway's advice, "Write as well as you can and finish what you begin." Don't let club memberships get in the way of your work. Whatever it is, your time can usually be put to much better and much more interesting use.

I believe that most people should never retire. Keep setting new and interesting goals as long as you live. Dr. Einstein, after a life of unprecedented achievement, was working on his unified theory when the end caught up with him. That he failed to complete it isn't as important from his standpoint as the fact that it kept him fully interested until the last day of his life.

Well-Balanced Life

Once a person has achieved a major goal, quite often in their late fifties or sixties, there's often a tendency to quit, to retire. With the last goal complete, we no longer have a compelling consuming interest. Our work has been done. Unless we've lived a well-balanced life and found many interests outside our work, we can upon the completion of a major goal, find ourselves sinking into depression with a sudden awareness of our mortality.

Unless a new interest is found or a subsidiary interest as an offshoot of the goal just completed, we can find ourselves settling down in apathy and boredom and it can be fatal. It can take years off our life, years that might otherwise be enjoyed to the fullest.

Lifetime learning is becoming more important today than ever. A competent person involved in consistent improvement will be the leaders today and tomorrow. We look to leaders for direction and we should take care when deciding which leaders to follow.

Of course, we call this conformity. The business suggests going along, doing what most other people are doing without clearly thinking too much about it. It is the most natural thing in the world to emulate the people with whom we come in contact. That is act, talk, and generally conduct ourselves the way our neighbors do. If they say a thing is so, we have a tendency to agree; and when our turn comes, repeat it.

Now I'm all for having a model to pattern our lives after if we want one, but what I'm suggesting is that we know where the person is going whom we're following. The trouble with just going blindly along doing what our neighbors are doing is that our neighbors may be heading toward someplace we won't like after we get there.

Then too, there's always the possibility that they might be following us while we think we're following them, and the result is that we're going around a full circle without anyone knowing where they are going.

People are funny. They don't like to be first as a rule.

Have you ever been at a dance and no one would get out on the floor until other people were already out there dancing? And have you ever thought, *What if everyone felt the same way? The band would play all night and nobody would be dancing.*

I've noticed at a traffic signal who wouldn't move forward even after the light turned green until someone else started. Well, as a fine old professor of journalism told me one time, "Pick the writer whose work you most admire, and then write the way he or she writes, working at writing until you feel your beginning to approach the excellence of the writer you so admire." Of course, he didn't mean to write about the same things or write the same stories, but rather emulate the way the person wrote. And I think the same rule should apply to living successfully.

Life is more than going along to get along.

An Admirable Person

I think each young person should have a model, a person whom we admire so much we'd like to live our lives the way this person lived. The model could be someone who lived a long time ago in history. Or could be a person in our community, but should always be a person who's outstanding in some regard.

And that doesn't always not necessarily mean our neighbors. It never means conforming with the crowd because almost always the person we admire most was an exceptional person, right? An unusually fine and successful person in some respect. If there's any one thing you can say about any person we admire very much and whom we'd like to emulate, it's that the person was or is different from the majority.

So what it boils down to is that we don't really want to just follow the crowd at all, now do we? But if we're not careful, that's exactly what we'll spend our lives doing and winding up the same place the crowd does. We must take time to clearly think about our lives, our futures.

An Assignment

Now I have an assignment for you.

Get a sheet of paper, a ruler, and a pen or pencil. Now with the ruler, draw a line 9 inches long on the sheet of paper, we'll call that a person's lifeline. Each inch of that line represents 10 years. With a line 9 inches long, representing a lifespan of 90 years, the first 2 inches of the line represent 20 years, so draw a little vertical line 2 inches from the beginning of the line. These are the formative years, these first 20 are the years when we lay the groundwork for much of what is to follow.

Now, when you look at a line 9 inches long with just the first 2 inches marked off of the vertical line, you get a pretty good objective view of the fact that those first 2 inches or 20 years represent only about 22 percent of a lifetime. Yet the remainder 78 percent is to a large extent dependent on what we do with those first 20.

Now, we might not know what we want to do as adults. We might be completely confused and in the dark about our ultimate career, but whatever line we choose, regardless of what it might be, will be helped by a good education. A good education cannot possibly hurt us, while the lack of a good education can most definitely hurt us regardless of our ultimate choice.

This is not to say that education and training stop after 20 years. Far from it. I feel certain that most of what a person knows by the age 45 has been learned out of school. But those first 20 years often exert an enormous influence on the years that ought to follow. To a youngster, getting to be 20 years old or 21 seems like an eternity. Yet the average man works for 40 years after leaving school, often much longer. As Alexander Clark put it, "Let us watch well our beginnings, and results will manage themselves."

Continuing our topic of competency, let's think clearly about dealing with tough times that end up with a win.

Tough Times and Security

If you think times are bad now, imagine living in a tent city when you were only 10 years old. That's the life I experienced during the Great Depression. Nevertheless, out of such circumstances, competent people were ready, willing, and able to act on their ideas.

What's holding you back? Even though you're doing what you can to become competent, there's lots of evidence across all media that times are tough—yet problem times are times of unlimited possibilities for competent people.

During the very worst years of the Great Depression is when the American film industry really got it together. And William Wrigley evolved from selling soap, to baking soda, to chewing gum—building his business into the largest gum manufacturer in the world. During the national financial downfall, miniature golf, monopoly, and radio became popular. What a time for the entrepreneur, and it was the very time!

Despite the worst doldrums the nation had ever experienced from a fiscal standpoint, it produced the beginnings of thousands of companies that are today among the giants of the world. And there were also many, despite the opportunities, despite the options that failed, never to appear again.

All those auto companies, for example. There was a Pierce-Arrow at one time and a REO Flying Cloud, all now in the big garage in the sky. Unfortunately, the decision to become an entrepreneur, like the decision to marry, does not at the same time confer upon the person making the decision a burst of improvement in the intelligence department. Entrepreneurial activity is not an escape from discipline. It is in fact the exact opposite.

Mental Clarity

Thinking and focusing clearly is the highest function of the human being. We're apparently the only creatures on planet Earth that can do that. That's our bag and that's what we're here to do. We're here to think and solve problems and create and serve others by satisfying their needs.

When you sit down and begin to think about a problem, you are engaging in the highest function of which any known living creature on the planet can perform. There's nothing you can do that's better for you to do than think, and yet it's the very last thing the majority of people will do.

Most ask their neighbors for advice, the people at work, the people sitting next to them on the subway or downtown bus or airplane. Some people even seek the counsel of their in-laws before they will quietly and alone with pad and pencil sit down and think about a problem that confronts them.

I urge you to get away from where you are by taking the time to stop and think—and soon you will be moving forward to solving each and every problem that comes along the way.

THINKING CLEARLY

What thinking skills are you using to become a more strategic thinker?

_____

_____

_____

_____

_____

_____

_____

_____

_____

_____

_____

_____

_____

_____

_____

What skills or habits can you start this week
that will improve your mental clarity?

_____
_____
_____
_____
_____
_____
_____
_____
_____
_____
_____
_____
_____
_____
_____
_____
_____
_____

Write down some examples
of admirable people.

_____

_____

_____

_____

_____

_____

_____

_____

_____

_____

_____

_____

_____

_____

_____

_____

_____

_____

_____

What qualities and attributes make
them admirable to you?

_____

_____

_____

_____

_____

_____

_____

_____

_____

_____

_____

_____

_____

_____

_____

_____

_____

_____

_____

_____

2

SOLVING PROBLEMS

*Is strategic thinking a routine part
of how you solve problems?*

The Strangest Secret book became the first ever spoken word recording to sell more than a million copies and earn a gold record. One point that needs to be made about that message is the fact that the idea of recording a bestseller wasn't even part of the initial goal. It was simply an answer to a problem. It solved my problem of being in two places at the same time.

As told in *The Secret Advantage,* Strangest Secret Series Book 4:

> In 1956, I was retiring from a very busy schedule and had decided to take it easy for a while in Arizona. Since I'd be away, the manager of one of my businesses asked me if I would record on tape a message he could play at the next sales meeting.

This made sense to me, so I decided to put a 30-minute talk in capsule form the important things I'd learned during the more than 20 years of research on why men and women succeeded or failed in life. I spent quite a bit of time putting it together, and then I recorded the message and called it *The Strangest Secret*. It wasn't long before people started asking for copies of the tape. Eventually we had it pressed into a record.

At first, hoping that I might get back the cost of producing it—the masters, pressings, the record jacket, the artwork, the plates and all that—I just arbitrarily set a price of $15 on the record. I figured that helping people would be worth $15. And if it didn't help, they could certainly get their money back by returning it.

Well, to my amazement, *The Strangest Secret* started selling faster than ever. I soon had back my original investment, and immediately dropped the price on the record from $15 to $4.95. Then things really began to happen. My office had trouble keeping an adequate inventory. The record began to sell in the tens of thousands, and in a couple of years we'd sold more than a hundred

thousand copies to companies and individuals and countries all worldwide.

Problems produce great ideas and ideas are the foundation of all success—and the good news is that ideas
are free—and proficient, clear-thinking people know how
to solve problems.

Have you ever been reading and suddenly a sentence or paragraph jumps off the page and hits you right
between the eyes like a hammer? Well here's a sentence
I ran across sometime back that stopped me. There's
nothing particularly unusual or profound about it. Maybe
it won't affect you at all, but it did me. It was written by a
man named Robert Seashore, chairman of Department
of Psychology at Northwestern University: *The happiest
people are not the people without problems. They are the
people who know how to solve their problems.* Now that's
the kind of sentence that really starts me thinking.

People who seem to spend most of their time hang-
ing onto the short end of the stick will tell you that it's
because of their problems. Successful people have the
identical problems, but instead of complaining about
them, or if they do complain about them, they solve
them. So the problem isn't problems.

I wonder how many millions of people have sat at
their desks kicking their feet up and down and waving
their arms, all because they have problems they think

are standing between them and the things they want, and the things they want to do. They don't realize that problems are universal. Problems don't pick out any one person to frustrate or stymie. Problems distribute themselves without favor all worldwide.

So it all boils down to a matter, not of problems at all, but of people. That's what it always comes back to.

Problem-Solving Methods

There are several ways of trying to solve problems, but two main ways. The first is the *hectic or panic method.* Some people want to solve their problems so fast, they just jump at the first thing that pops into their minds without considering it very much—like a bird knocking against a pane of glass, these people fly around in circles. The *trial and error method* is when one thing won't work, they try another. Sometimes it works, particularly if the problem is simple; but more often than not, this is the long way around. It generally results in a lot of wasted time, a lot of worry, and sleepless nights.

The experts claim that it's possible to learn a definite system of problem solving that fits most problem situations. Instead of jumping from one thing to another, think through each solution to its possible outcome before you do anything about it. In other words, *the solution is a*

mentally thought-through method all the way to its possible
conclusion before it's tried.

There are six steps to solving problems:

- One, write your problem on paper.
- Two, list the obstacles standing in the way of solving it.
- Three, list the assets in favor of your solving the problem.
- Four, list as many possible solutions as you can think of—take your time doing this.
- Five, try to figure out the results of each solution.
- Six, choose the solution that seems best to you and put it into action. Stay with it long enough for it to work or prove that it won't. If it finally doesn't, choose another possible solution.

This is the scientific way to solve problems. Without problems, there would be no progress. Every success began with a problem to solve, and every business began with an idea to solve that problem.

These days we hear a lot about big business and how big it's getting. There's nothing wrong with big business, and one of the most interesting things about it is that every business, no matter how big it might be today,

Think through each solution to its possible outcome before you do anything about it.

started small. One of the largest corporations in the United States was started with about $30,000 of borrowed money, and after 10 years of operation only had $6,000 in its account.

But a good thing to remember too is that every business, no matter how big or far-flung, no matter how many thousands of employees in skyscraper office buildings it might have, got its start in the mind of one human being.

Committees are all right and groups are all right when it comes to solving problems, but every good idea had to start in the mind of one human being, and usually came as a result of something that person observed.

You could start a business of your own this year, which in 20 or 30 years could be a big, far-flung business too. People who tell you all the good businesses are taken or that there aren't any opportunities anymore are full of hot air—and I have to admit that there are quite a few of these people running around. They make you want to come out with Shakespeare's classic line, "He jests at scars that never felt a wound."

Solve the Filling-a-Need Problem

There are six words that lie at the root of any business success: *Find a need, and fill it.* The extent of your success will be determined by your ability to think strategically how to fill that need and by the need's importance.

Anytime you see a business thriving and successful, you must realize that it is filling a need. If it weren't, it would just stop and close up shop—the size of a business is controlled only by the number of people it serves.

For example, a store that can accommodate 500 people must be larger than a business that can accommodate only 100. I know a man who made a really big business running a gas station. One day he was watching a customer and noticed that while the customer's car was being serviced, he just stood around and waited. The man probably had money to spend, and there were undoubtedly things he'd like to buy, things he needed—if they were available.

So my friend started adding these items, and he kept right on adding them until he had to add a big sporting goods store alongside of the now large and modern gas station. While your car is being serviced at his station, you can buy anything from a package of chewing gum to a $200 shotgun, or a boat and trailer, outboard motor, a box of chocolates for your wife. Customers can also cash a check anytime they feel like it, and he extends credit on everything. On a Friday or Saturday, he cashes $40 to $50,000 worth of checks on each day, and hardly anyone leaves without buying something, or at least having their car serviced.

My friend's business was no different from any other gas station in the country, but he *thought* about his business, and one day there popped into his mind an idea.

He saw a need and he filled it. The fact is, there's more opportunity today, far more than there ever was before. We're completely surrounded by it. There's just one catch to it. We have to be able to see it. A lot of people would like to try something better, but they're security conscious and worried. There's no way in the world to get to second base unless you take your foot off first.

Getting on base wins games. It's not always the home runs. Becoming competent is a journey, a long list of experiences that makes you capable to stay on course for the long run to success.

The Quest

One of the most interesting things about people is that each one has to make a journey never before made by any human being on earth. Do you ever think about that? The journey, or odyssey really since it's usually a series of journeys, is the quest for our self. Since we are unlike any person who ever lived, our road must cover unexplored ground.

I wonder how many people feel within themselves a restless energy, a great driving force that seeks expression, but who do not know or have not found the proper area or channel for its expression. They know and rightly so, that there's something that it's meant for them to do, and that if they could find it, they would do it surpassingly

There's no way in the world to get to second base unless you take your foot off first.

well. They would find the perfect outlet for all their energies, talents, and abilities that are now dammed up within them.

I suppose there are two possible courses of action for such people. They can stay with what they are now doing, bank the fires that burn within, and hope they'll eventually cool and die as I believe they will. Or they can set out on the journey to find the world that was meant for them to live, because of their aptitudes and abilities. For every person, there is an area in which they can excel.

If you take a sheet of paper, and starting at one edge, begin to draw a horizontal line. As you get near the center of the page, draw a rounded hill above the plane, and then finish your line on the same plane on the page where it began. That hill can be said to represent your strongest area, the area of your greatest potential. Some people work on the sides of the hill, some near the bottom, and probably millions on the flat plane below. The most fortunate people are those who have found expression at the highest point of that hill, right at the top, where they can use their greatest strengths—and as a result, reap their greatest harvest.

Now turn the page upside down. Instead of a hill rising above a plane, you have a canal. The cross section of a canal. It reaches its greatest depth in the exact center, doesn't it? And it's here where you can sail the largest ship. As you near the edges, the water gets shallower and only small craft can move safely there. The largest ships can sail anywhere in the world with ease and safety. The smaller craft must hug the shoreline. Each of us has or is the large ship, but we must find the channel in which we can reach our greatest depth. The right channel for us.

This is the most exciting quest—the journey to find ourselves and our fulfillment as persons. When we've reached our destination, we'll know that we've arrived—for then we'll do with ease and ability what others deem difficult, if not impossible. Instead of dreading our work or being bored by it, we'll find it interesting, challenging, and greatly rewarding. It's the work right for us to do.

For every person, there is an area in which they can excel.

Since a journey to any place must begin where we now are, each of us is now on the road. We can stay where we are or follow it. It seems to me that a lifetime is far too short a period and too precious to be spent doing something we don't like to do, and for which we have little aptitude. Both the person and humankind as a whole are the losers.

Define the Problem

So first, we need to know how to solve problems that we may be facing that are hindering out journey, our quest to find fulfillment.

First, define the problem. "A problem defined as half solved," as the saying is, and it's true. Just seeing the problem spelled out helps to clarify it. Then we can start writing down possible solutions and we can put down the pencil or pen and stare off into space as we turn the problem over and over in our mind, like a chicken on a rotisserie, exposing every part of it to the radiance of our mind and the great powers to which the mind has recourse.

Over and over we turn it and we write down everything possible we can think of that might lead to its solution, no matter how silly it might appear to others who will never see it. We keep this to ourselves and we keep looking for answers. Then we ask, are there any books on the subject that might be helpful?

Surely other people have had the same problem. Let's see what they did about it. Are there experts we can contact on the subject now? That's the sort of counsel we want. And if we think it's a good idea, let's talk it over with someone whose ideas we respect and we can count for serious help on the matter. And as we crank our rotisserie and consider the problem, we keep a positive attitude about it.

We look at the problem as a challenge, something to solve and overcome, not as something that will continue

Look at problems as a challenge to solve and overcome, not something that blocks you.

to block us. We know there's an answer. What is it? And one fine day as we're taking a stroll or a shower or driving the car or even sleeping, almost always at our leisure, the solution to our problem will appear. It'll appear with all the lovely clarity of an elk on the far bank of a mountain lake—and when it does, we write it down and we continue to write about it.

And when it's as clearly defined as we can make it, we try to push farther and see if there are more good solutions lurking just behind it. Sometimes the first answer is a kind of teaser and there are better ideas further on. So let's push on writing down whatever else comes to us, and we've solved the problem for the time being. When we've done that, we've accomplished what we were designed to do. We have solved a problem.

Two Kinds of Problems

Of course, there are two kinds of problems. There are *convergent problems* and there are *divergent problems.* Convergent problems are those which as the word implies converge, that is two or more factors can be brought together for different directions, which when brought to an intersection, solve the problem. Building a house is such a problem, and when all the parts are in place, the house is complete. The problem has been successfully solved. All physical problems, or perhaps I should say mechanical problems are ultimately convergent.

Divergent problems deal with other human beings. How to educate people is a divergent problem because what will work for one person won't necessarily work for another. Living successfully in marriage is a divergent problem, and one that must be solved on a daily basis.

Each day we begin all over again and solve the problems of that day. And even mechanical problems when solved are very temporary because of the factor of change. The changes in transportation are a good example or the changes in communication. What solves the problem today will not necessarily provide the solution a year or two from now or three years from now.

High-tech products are on an order of change measured by three years. In three years, the new product we're using will be improved upon sufficiently to bring up the question of replacement. Each time we solve a problem, we increase our capacity to solve the next one as well as our attitude toward problems in general.

Daily Doable Problems

If you're a creative genius with little affection or aptitude for keeping books, for example, solving that problem is to make sure you enlist someone you both trust and know to be competent in the areas of your incompetence. Or contract for such services and make the daily examination of the books part of your regimen, no matter how dull or uninteresting you may find it. Ignorance is unfortunately no excuse for failure or solving a solvable problem. You can learn to read a financial statement and assess your accounts receivable even if your hair grows to your shoulders.

America has always been a paradise to thousands of worried, harried, struggling entrepreneurs. The word "paradise" will no doubt bring a wry smile or perhaps an earthy expletive commonly heard on the docks. For thousands of once-hopeful companies, chapter 11 seems like the only way out, reorganization for the benefit of creditors, and not much benefit at that. There are no guarantees. Don't confuse opportunity with guarantee.

And it's best you get rid of that terrible word "security," now, once and for all. There's no such thing as security as long as you're alive. Dead, you're secure. Unborn, you're secure. If you're alive, you are the very epitome of insecurity.

Think about it, you're on a small planet hurtling through space, the mystery of space, at about a million miles an hour. The dinosaurs were here for millions of years and were far more successful as living creatures than we've been with our short-lived appearances—yet they were extinguished in a matter of weeks because of a giant meteor that raised so much dust it obliterated the sun, and they froze to death.

Security, there's no such thing. But there is opportunity, there is joy, there is love. There are all kinds of

Each time we
solve a problem,
we increase
our capacity to
solve the next
one as well as
our attitude
toward problems
in general.

wonderful things to do and see and experience—but there's no security whatsoever. You can call an 80-year existence in the billions of years the universe has been around security. In one way, we are. We're secure in our foreknowledge of the time we have and we can see how well we can use that time. But the kind of security most people are looking for, that's something else.

Ask Yourself

Ask yourself, "What do I want to do with my time, however short or long it may be? Do I want to make it big? Do I want to see the world and live in a penthouse apartment overlooking the sea and drive fine European cars, and command a 50-foot flybridge fishing boat with twin diesels throbbing below my feet? Or do I want to make a difference with what I believe to be a very good idea or talent that I've worked very hard to hone to marketability? If the money comes, great, I can spend it as well as the next guy, but I'm happiest doing my thing, and I don't want a boss telling me what to do for the rest of my working life. I want to be independent as much as that's possible, considering I can only succeed to the extent that I serve others. My public, whatever that amounts to, is my boss. I must please those people or they won't give me the money to buy the things I need and want."

Elementary, my dear Watson.

If we have just a small amount of time to live, who would want to spend it tiptoeing through life, trying to make it safely to death?

Lots of people.

Short time, long time. Most people get very nervous when they think of being in charge of their own economic well-being. They want that check every week. The one with the great name at the top that makes everyone glad to catch it. And don't knock it, that's where your own key people will come from. If they were all in business for themselves, there'd be a heck of a lot more competition than there is. And keep in mind that competition only exists at all if you choose to play follow the leader. Rolls-Royce isn't in competition with anyone, neither is Mercedes-Benz, really. Take a look at IBM and the rest of the top cats, people at the top of their lines of business, nope, they're not concerned about competition. They're too busy creating.

If you are a pacesetter, you're not competing, you're leading, you're creating. You've carved your own niche out of the market like Poggenpohl kitchens or Baker Furniture. My company, the Nightingale-Conant Corporation of Chicago, doesn't have any competitors. We have copiers, sure, that's the sincerest form of flattery. But competitors, no. We never will have as long as we have the gung-ho creative management we have and the team that puts it all together. You won't see us on

Fortune's list of the top 500 corporations in America, but we're number one in our industry. We founded it.

The one big idea that started Nightingale-Conant was The Strangest Secret program. I had discovered that secret in one of the many books that I read during those years of the Depression. I found the secret in Napoleon Hill's book *Think and Grow Rich,* and the secret was these six words: "We become what we think about."

Yes, we become what we think about, but the thinking is up to us—and the degree to which people regularly underestimate their capacity for accomplishment is immeasurable. We think nothing of the accomplishments of others. That is what others do, we take in stride.

But when it comes to setting goals for ourselves, we tend to play things outrageously safe and thus remain within limits embarrassingly small, especially if there's some sort of maintenance program in effect. That is if we have a job though its real demands upon us are minimal, we'll usually shut down any other efforts to prepare ourselves for: number one, a much better, more interesting kind of work; and two, any sudden emergency that might develop.

I remember watching a television news program in which laid-off workers of a closed navy yard were being interviewed. The announcer asked, "What are you men going to do now that the navy yard is closed down?"

The man nearest to him said, "Well, I guess we'll just have to wait for it to reopen again."

Another man said, "I've worked in this navy yard for 25 years. I don't know anything else."

In 25 years, a person could learn to do heart transplants in his spare time. What were all these people doing with the 16 hours a day they were not working? What about weekends and vacations?

Take a pen and paper and work out the number of hours the average working person is actually on the job during a typical year, then subtract it from the rest of

We become what we think about—and the thinking is up to us.

his or her waking time. If an hour a day were devoted to learning anything valuable, the ending of a job would be an incidental thing or an actual benefit.

And how about "strategic think time"? Anyone who's responsible for providing for a family should have emergency plans A, B, and C. At least A. A platoon leader in combat must ask, "What if the enemy attacks at night, from the rear, on Sunday morning during breakfast?" The family provider should ask and work out on that legal pad, "What do we do if the company I work for goes out of business or lets me go for any reason?" It's the kind of thinking that a couple can do together, as well as separately, and as a result have several possible courses of action.

And in the meantime, how about that educational program in your main field of interest? During the industrial shakeout of the early 1980s, we heard this comment again and again, "I worked for that company for 30 years and now I'm out, just like that." To hear them talking, one might think they had made a personal sacrifice for the welfare of the company they worked for. They say nothing about the fact that the company paid them for their time at the job and gave them the wherewithal to become anything they might set their hearts upon becoming.

It was a fair arrangement. They were not kidnapped and pressed into servitude. They applied for their jobs and were accepted and were paid for the level of work they performed. There was no agreement to provide them with work until they were too old and infirm to continue. Why didn't they take the possibility of a layoff into consideration and prepare for such an emergency?

Prepare for Problems

John and Elsie did. When John was laid off, he and Elsie sold their home in Ohio and moved to Florida, where they retired in the sunshine. If he'd been laid off years sooner, they had their little real estate refurbishing business on the side they could have turned to full-time. If they had, they would've gotten rich. The trouble with John and Elsie was that they, like so many of us, underestimated what they could do at the time he was devoting to his job at the steel mill.

The job and the regular weekly paycheck was something such people just don't voluntarily give up very often, but such men had father or mother figures on whom they depended for safety as well as survival. One was the union, the other was the company. The company was so big, with such big smokestacks, and employed so many people and made so much steel or whatever. Well, it had been there forever, and it would remain, and all they had to do was show up, do whatever was necessary to keep the job, and then go home again.

Why did no one talk to these people about change? How do such people remain isolated from important information? "Keep reading like that and you'll ruin your eyes," I used to hear my father say. Reading doesn't hurt the eyes, it's good for them, and especially good for what's lurking just behind them. But of course, all that's gradually changing. Each year, more people move into the group that thinks.

As you move into the group that thinks and becomes more competent, the risks will seem smaller. The idea that results in a person running the risks of starting his or her own business depends strictly upon the person, the person's background, education, previous level of accomplishment, and aspirations.

For most of us, going into business is a pursuit beset by many problems, irritations, headaches, sleepless nights, long hours, and low pay. Yes, being in business for yourself does not necessarily mean an inordinately high income, on the contrary. It often means very little or no income at all for long periods of time. But once the business hits, whether it takes five years or fifteen, you then have the world by the tail. You decide what you're worth in the salary and bonus departments and the company can pay for much that would ordinarily come out of an employee's pay.

On becoming truly successful, it usually takes longer than we realize when we begin. Like the decision to have a child, we seldom take into consideration the length and arduous nature of the contract. But if our idea is sound and if we are sound and if we fully understand the concept of service and the importance of working capital and constant upgrading of our product or service, and if we have the perseverance of Columbus, we'll wake up some fine morning to find ourselves one of the competent ones of our generation. We've achieved a kind of independence never known or perhaps understood by the employee, no matter how high he or she may travel in the hushed corridors of executive country.

America's top executives working for large multinational corporations usually earn more in salary and perks, stock options and bonuses than the great majority of entrepreneurs. But the entrepreneur has something else—control. And once the business is truly successful, which means it's probably in a state of happy expansion, he or she can hire the best executives to run things while he or she takes a few months rest in Hawaii, Augusta, or plays golf in Nairobi, and does a bit of deep sea fishing in the Seychelles.

"You say it might take fifteen years for that kind of success?"

"Yes, I do." But how long would it take you if you worked for Sysco Foods or Chrysler?

"Fifteen or twenty years, I suppose, if ever."

Right. And the fifteen years aren't all pain, suffering and sleepless nights. There's a lot of joy in there too. There's the joy of seeing your own ideas in action and of watching your own ideas and efforts win against the competition. There's the joy of watching the money pour in along with the orders. There's a sort of kindly vindication in that.

I resigned from CBS and station WBBM in Chicago in March 1950. My friends at WBBM told me repeatedly what an idiot I was. I had reached the top. I went to work in the beautifully paneled brass trimmed elevators of the world-famous Wrigley building in Chicago. I rubbed shoulders with the rich and famous and I earned top dollar in my profession. Thousands, no millions listened while I read the news or read the latest Jello commercial. Man, I was on top of the heap. I had it made—and I was only 28 years old.

Bouncing Back

You've probably heard the expression, "You can't keep a good man down." Well, you can't. You can take a good man and completely wipe him out, take everything but his mind and his spirit and a wife who's willing to start over, and no matter where you put him, he'll come bouncing right back. In a year, he'll be back where he was when the ax fell.

You see, he has the only security a person can have— deep inside. His wife and kids can feel it when he sits down to the breakfast table with them. You can feel it whenever he enters a room, and you can see it by the way he walks down the street. He's an expert at his business and he knows it.

And while most men are doing just as little as they can to sneak by, he's working harder and studying and planning and growing with his industry and his country. He doesn't feed on the economy. He contributes to it. No matter what your job happens to be at this moment, it's loaded with opportunity.

If you think about your job and its application to its industry and our economy and constantly come up with ways to improve it, ways of becoming better at it, in an almost unbelievably short time you will be practically indispensable. The company will most probably give you more and more responsibility and need you even more when times are bad. You get the idea, I'm sure. This is security—and it's the only kind we can develop.

George Bernard Shaw once said, "I have no use for people who blame circumstances for their position in life. I like people who look for the circumstances they seek, and if they can't find them, make them." Do you know as much about your work as a doctor has to know about medicine or a lawyer about law? You should, you know. There are no good or bad jobs. It's all in the way we look at them.

Jobs don't have futures, people do. How many times have you heard someone say, "There's no future in this job"? Isn't it amazing that generation after generation, the great bulk of people never seem to understand that the job is not the problem? This "problem" is caused by people who know how to talk, but little else, passing nonsense down to their children and to their associates.

It's too bad there isn't an intelligence test given as one of the requirements for a marriage license. Not that we expect youngsters getting married to know a great deal at that stage of their lives. None of us did. But at least they should want to learn so that they could handle a responsibility of passing good information along to their children instead of warping their fine little minds with a lot of idiotic nonsense.

Jobs and the Future

There is no such thing as a job with or without a future. A job is a condition, a circumstance, nothing more. A job is neither good nor bad nor a problem. It's what we do with a job that makes it good or bad that gives it a future or keeps it from having one. Jobs don't have futures, people do.

And there's no such thing as a job that does not hold somewhere within it everything we could possibly want in the way of satisfaction and rewards if we'll make a great job out of it—solve the supposedly problem. But the majority of people it would seem are in reverse. They're fashioned by their jobs instead of realizing the importance of it being the other way around.

There is no such thing as a job with or without a future. Jobs don't have futures, people do.

People who get to the top of their business or profession held the very same positions at one time or another that people had said there was no future. And it seems that the simplest fact, once it's understood, lies at the root of the problem. The so-called average individual never seems to understand that what seems to be the easy way in the beginning is always the hardest way in the end—and what seems to be the hardest way in the beginning is always the easiest and best way in the end.

Most people take a job, do what they feel is expected of them, and that's the end of it. This seems like the easiest course of action. It's like a person coming to a large body of water deciding to go across and deciding that it's easier to swim than build a boat. So he simply jumps in and starts swimming. Long before he reaches the opposite shore, if he ever does, he'll wish he had taken the time to build a raft or a boat with a sail. It seems harder at first to build the boat. It takes time and extra work, little planning, but your chances of reaching the distant shore are a thousand times better.

And while the swimmers must call on more and more energy the farther out they get, you can sail along holding the tiller and steering a straight course toward your destination. Riding within the protection of the extra work and extra planning you took the time to create, your future is infinitely brighter, your trip far more comfortable.

If you're in work that you do believe does not have a future, it might mean you haven't really examined it or given it everything you've got. I think the army of young people coming out of college today, and in their naivete asking about the future of the job they seek, should remember the words: *Jobs don't have futures, people do.* Truer words were never spoken.

So what businesses are good to start and become successful? The question really should be, is there competent management in place to run the businesses successfully?

Starting a business and succeeding in it is, of course, difficult and takes a lot more time than most of us like to think about, but it offers a great future for men and especially women interested in heading their own enterprises. It's the one place where ancient prejudices about women can't get in their way. And not even the sky is the limit anymore these days.

About 35 percent[2] of all new entrepreneurs are women, but the unsuccessful serve in one important way. They are endless consumers. They buy and eat breakfast cereal and hamburgers and eggs and salad and bread and everything on every shelf of every store in the country. Individually, they do not consume nearly as much as successful people do, but their numbers are so great, they can buy so much laundry detergent and toothpaste

---

2. "Women started 49% of new businesses in the US in 2021, up from 28% in 2019," *World Economic Forum,* July 20, 2022; https://www.weforum .org/agenda/2022/07/women-entrepreneurs-gusto-gender/; accessed October 26, 2024.

and painkillers and shampoo, you wouldn't believe it, and cars and pickup trucks and vans and gasoline.

Alibis and Excuses

As human creatures, we all started even somewhere back there. In every family, somebody has to start the ball rolling if one of the members is to move from the ranks of the unsuccessful into the camp of the successful. Most people, especially the unsuccessful, live in tiny, tightly circumscribed worlds, just a neighborhood, really. Like sea anemones, they seem fastened to one place and manage to find sufficient nourishment for their needs.

Here's one of the ridiculous comments I used to hear as a child when I would ask an adult if he or she was interested in seeing other parts of the country. In those days, I wasn't even thinking about other parts of the world. They used to say in response, "I didn't lose anything there." That used to give me such a sinking feeling, as though the only reason anyone would ever go someplace different would be to find something they had lost.

Later and much older, I realized it was their pet alibi for not having achieved the means to travel. Another excuse for being miserable was that "Only poor people are happy." That was one I found particularly frustrating even at a very early age. *Why,* I would ask myself over and over again, *Why wouldn't rich people be happy?* It seemed to me they'd have every reason to be happy.

And there was an excuse made about the people who went to college or otherwise got themselves a good education. This one went like this, "Oh, sure, he's got a college education, but he hasn't got enough sense to come in out of the rain." Did you ever hear that one? Did you find it to be as ridiculous as I did? It was an oxymoron, a non sequitur. *If a person spent all that time getting an education,* I would ask myself, *why in the world wouldn't he have enough sense to come in out of the rain?* I decided to find out.

Successful people managed to be on top of things at least most of the time, and unsuccessful people are not; rather, things stay on top of them. They never take charge of their own lives and destiny. They don't set difficult goals for themselves. They don't seem to know enough. And of the great mountain range of information they don't have is the innocent fact that *we become what we think about.*

From "I'll Do Anything" to
"I'll Do Something"

In tough times, most people make a drastic mistake when it comes to how much they'll make.

Back during the depression of the 1930s when millions of Americans were daily forming long lines outside employment offices and no "Help Wanted" signs appeared in thousands of business windows, do you know what words were most often heard? Practically, all of the people looking for work said the same thing or a variation of the same theme, "Give me a job, I'll do anything." And that's why they had so much trouble finding work.

In the first place, the depression had put a crimp on most businesses. Thousands folded and those that remained through good management and necessary products and services were mostly cutting back on the number of employees, and were not looking for more. The one thing in the world they were *not* looking for was someone who said, "Give me a job. I'll do anything."

But a man I know solved the problem. He discovered how to get a job during the toughest part of the depression in just about any business he chose—and his method was surprisingly simple and logical.

When he found himself with millions of others out of a job and with a family to support, he seriously thought about it and asked himself, *What does the businessman need today more than anything else?* And the only logical answer to that was *more business.*

So my friend picked the line of business he was most interested in, and where he felt he could help the most. He then began studying that business. He spent weeks learning all he could about it. He went to a man in that business and posed as a man in the same business from out of town. Then he'd spent hours talking with the man about the business problems brought on by the depression and the shortage of money. He spent days in a public library learning all he could about that particular business. He spent this whole time strategically thinking—racking his brain for ideas that could be of help, ways and means of improving and increasing business in this particular line.

One of the most amazing things he learned was that his weeks of study, talking, and research ended with

Be the person on the white horse.

knowing as much and in some cases more about the business than some of the men he talked to. They were mostly waiting for something good to develop, and he was knocking himself out actively engaged in doing something about it himself.

To make a long story short, when he felt he was ready and he had gathered together some really good ideas on ways to increase business in this line, he then went to a stranger in that line of work and said something to the effect, "I believe I know of several ways in which your business can be increased and your profit picture improved. I'd like to work with you on it."

This man, who instead of asking for a job and saying he'd do anything, appeared as the man on the white horse with ways and means of helping keep a business alive and actually increasing profits. Needless to say, he got the job and he sailed through the depression without any more trouble.

You'd be surprised how many businesses are looking for someone on a white horse even today. But you'd also be surprised how few there are who are willing to become that person, who are willing to take the time and the necessary study and research to find ways to really helping a keep or enhance a business.

JOURNAL

SOLVING PROBLEMS

*Is strategic thinking a routine part
of how you solve problems?*

_____

_____

_____

_____

_____

_____

_____

_____

_____

_____

_____

_____

_____

_____

_____

_____

What is your initial reaction
to most problems?

_____

_____

_____

_____

_____

_____

_____

_____

_____

_____

_____

_____

_____

_____

_____

_____

_____

_____

*Think about and write down some problems
you have solved or solve on a daily basis.*

_____

_____

_____

_____

_____

_____

_____

_____

_____

_____

_____

_____

_____

Do you find satisfaction in solving them?

_____

_____

_____

_____

What are some ways to see
problems as challenges?

_____

_____

_____

_____

_____

_____

_____

_____

_____

_____

_____

_____

_____

_____

_____

_____

_____

_____

3

IMAGINING CREATIVELY

*Are you creatively imagining
as a strategic thinker?*

Most Americans are not nearly as creative as they could be. They just go through the motions of the job. They do what they have to and no more. They waste a large share of their time daydreaming, watching the clock, wishing that days were done. Because they think of putting in a certain number of hours instead of producing something of value, these people never really develop the creative talents they have, and the loss to society is enormous. They lose, their employers lose, and society in general loses the great wealth that could flow from these creative minds.

If you're an executive or a creative worker of any kind, such as artists, writers, researchers, inventors and so on, anyone who is primarily engaged in creative work probably makes a serious mistake if they attempt to work more than about six hours a day. For when they do, their minds are not likely to have enough time to digest problems and subconsciously solve them in its own leisurely fashion.

Yes, we've found with monotonous regularity that any time creative workers get so busy doing things that they haven't enough time to think about, they do not get many creative ideas. They just get tired.

Studies indicate that even though a creative worker is able to work for approximately six hours a day or even more without losing creativity, it's not a good idea for workers to make a general practice of pressing themselves to this limit. It's far better to work about four hours a day, when they are really on top of things and can approach maximum productivity and effectiveness. And under these conditions, the creative worker always has reserved power to meet an emergency. So then, all the results of the study suggest that, even in an emergency, if creative workers work more than about six hours a day, they likely will defeat their own purposes.

In summing up, there's an excellent chance that you can be of more value to yourself, your family, and to society if you can find a way to be tremendously effective four hours a day, rather than just putting in eight.

Imagination

A big important word for competent thinkers: *imagination.*

The statistics vary, but most experts, universities and so on, agree that most of us are operating somewhere between 10 percent and 25 percent of our abilities. This covers about everything we do, but there's one department where this can really hurt us, and this department is labeled *imagination.*

There's the true story of two men who, at about the same age, opened stores on the same street of the same town. Both these men were honest, thrifty, and industrious. Twenty years later, one of the men owned a store about a hundred times as big as the one he originally started. The other man was still having a tough time keeping his head above water in the same shop he had started with. So the question is, "What's the difference between the two men?" According to the experts, the whole difference is a thing called imagination. You don't really need the story of the two stores to realize the truth of what imagination will do.

Every day, thousands of people are starting out pretty even with just about the same equipment, the same backgrounds, and so forth. Some will go farther, have more fun and excitement out of life, do more, see more, experience more, and wind up with more. Those who do, whether they realized it or not, are using their imagination being a faculty of their mind. Imagination is free and everyone on earth has the same crack at it, but some use it more than others.

Imagination is free and everyone on earth has the same crack at it, but some use it more than others.

The great Charles F. Kettering once said, "Where there's an open mind, there will always be a frontier." So what it all comes down to is that how a person uses his or her imagination can mean the difference between making the grade or not making it. By following Mr. Kettering's advice and keeping an open mind, the imagination gets a chance to do a little work on its own.

After your imagination has come up with an idea, a negative impulse will generally come into the picture. Fear is the almost automatic reaction to imagination. It seems that as soon as we get an idea, we begin to wonder what others will think of it; and since most people don't have too high an opinion of themselves, we start tearing our own idea to pieces with the usual result that we discard it entirely. Then a couple of years later, we hear about someone who has been very successful with the idea we tossed into the ash can. So we console themselves by telling people we actually got the idea first, but didn't do anything with it. It's not much consolation, is it?

Once the imagination has come up with a good idea, a sound idea, it then takes two other ingredients to round out the picture. The first is *courage,* and the second is *stubborn determination.* Children have these qualities or they would never learn to walk. In the process of learning to walk, they fall a thousand times and ram their little heads into tables and walls, but they keep wobbling up again until they finally get the hang of it. Adults as a group are different, a couple of falls and they've had it.

Imagination is really nothing more than vision, which has been responsible for everything that's happened in the world. Without this one aspect of ourselves, we'd still be peeking out of caves. Fortunately for all of us, there are enough men and women with the courage to stick with their vision and imagination to keep us moving along. But while you're thinking about it, you might rate yourself in the imagination, courage, and determination. Like the two men with stores on the same street, your vision can make a lot of difference.

Imagination is really nothing more than vision.

Communicating with Others

How you communicate with others illustrates how far along you are to becoming a strategic thinker. It's been said that people with small minds talk about other people. People with average minds talk about things. And people with excellent minds talk about ideas.

It's true that the greatest minds the world has produced were most interested, most obsessed by ideas rather than by things or people, even though their ideas affected people and things. What do you talk about in your conversations? Are you most concerned about other people, things such as say cars, boats, or ballgames, or do you mostly talk about ideas or ways of improving your lot in life or the betterment of your community or whatever it happens to be?

If you find that your conversation usually centers on people, people who are not present during the conversation, your mind could probably stand some improvement. You're wasting your time; but more important, you're wasting your mind.

You're using the greatest tool on the face of the earth on subjects far beneath its capabilities. If most of your conversation centers on things such as a new car or a kitchen stove or the batting averages of your favorite ballplayers, your mind is rather average. Now of course all of these things will occupy our conversation part of the time. We're bound to talk about people and about things.

But it's what you talk about *most* of the time that determines how you think and what kind of a person you are.

I think everybody should have a cause, an idea that's important to you, that should occupy most of you thinking and conversation. What's your cause? What are you working toward in life? What is it that you're enthusiastic and excited about? If you have to say there's nothing you're working toward and looking forward to with excitement and anticipation, you are missing most of the fun of living.

It's what you talk about most of the time that determines how you think and what kind of a person you are.

I know people who have retired from business in their seventies and eighties. One of them is the retired chairman of the board of one of the country's largest corporations, and these people are just as busy, just as vital, as vibrant and interested today in what they're now doing as they were fifty years ago when they were first fashioning their business careers, careers that were outstandingly successful.

Every human being needs something worthwhile to look forward to and to work toward—and if they are not, they will operate traditionally far below their capabilities. Life becomes rather humdrum, and thoughts turn more and more inward, more and more on themselves. A man or woman with a cause can forget themselves, can lose themselves within the larger picture, which fills their lives with challenge and interest.

At any rate, I encourage you to check your conversation from time to time, see if you're spending most of your time or rather wasting most of your time talking about other people or about things that aren't really too important. Or are you thinking about ideas, are you using your imagination to work toward bringing those ideas to life?

In considering the power of attitude and imagination, a good quote by a psychologist is, "There is a deep tendency in human nature to become precisely like that which you habitually imagine yourself to be."

If you're not
working toward
and looking
forward to
something with
excitement and
anticipation,
you're missing
most of the
fun of living.

Visualization

Imagination plays a big role in the topic of *visualization.*

It does little good to remonstrate, or bicker with an entrepreneur. For example, Christopher Columbus, brilliant navigator that he was, could have spent his life in peace navigating up and down the coastal waters of Europe and remaining within the known boundaries of the period's world maps.

But at the edges of the known waters, there appeared the terrifying legend, "Here, there be dragons." And it was there that Columbus desired to sail and it's there that every entrepreneur desires to sail. It's interesting to note that on the maps beyond the known world, there was never a legend reading, "Here, there be unlimited opportunity for exploration." No doubt there may have been much gold and silver and precious gems and strange human creatures living beyond these boundaries, waiting to be discovered and developed—for the daring and intrepid sailor, like Columbus.

Even though it had always been that way out there beyond the horizon, no one ever suggested that it might be that way. It's the natural proclivity of cartographers and advice givers to look upon the unknown as bad. For they, like children going into a darkened basement alone, feel that the dark and the unknown must hold strange and fearful creatures unimaginable in the known and lighted world. They cannot think otherwise, it's their nature.

Yet at the time of Columbus, not a single live dragon had ever been seen upon the planet Earth by anyone. Dragons were in fact fairytale creatures, yet they always inhabited the uncharted regions of the world—depicted as such right on the maps.

Let It Simmer

So when you use your imagination and get an idea that you think will result in an excellent business of your own, and it needn't be a new idea by any means, keep it to

Times are not bad, it's just a tendency to let fear create bad thoughts about the times.

yourself and your secret notepad for a period of time while you simmer it on the rotisserie of your mind's consciousness and unconsciousness. Let it turn while you view it from every angle. Look at it from the standpoint of the worst possible scenario. If it's a good, sound idea, it should survive even the worst times, as good businesses do.

Incidentally, there are recession-free businesses and many businesses that do better in recessions than in good times. Again, that proves that times are not bad, it's just a tendency to let fear create bad thoughts about the times that we are in. Strategic people always find security and become indispensable by focus. It goes a long way toward proving the importance of specialization. I don't mean a person should specialize to the point of closing your mind to everything else in the world. In fact, the best specialists are those who have a wide range of general knowledge as a platform for their specialty. But I am saying that it pays to know how to do one thing exceedingly well.

In first place, none of us can be good at everything, and the best answer to that is to become outstanding at one thing and know a little about everything. Henry Ford once said, "If money is your only hope for independence, you will never have it. The only real security we can have in this world is a reserve of knowledge, experience, and ability." He was right.

Concentrate on one endeavor, learn all you can about it, get experience in that line—and you build a lifetime of security.

And a good part of this knowledge, experience, and ability should be in one field. You see, by concentrating on one line of endeavor and really learning all you can about it and getting all the experience you can in that line, you are building the kind of security that lasts a lifetime. And if you go about it the right way, you can be recognized as a real authority in a few years. You become as close to being indispensable as a person can become—and you can go sailing through economic ups and downs without too much trouble or danger.

In fact, the rougher the economic waters become, the more you're needed to help the ship sail back into calm waters again. A business is a lot like a ship, when it's in dangerous of sinking, everything goes over the side, every bit of spare gear, everything except what is vital for its safety and the safety of the passengers. So the more vital a person, your ability and knowledge become to the successful operation of a job or business, the less chance of your being jettisoned when things get rough.

Economists estimate that the next ten to twenty years, barring thermonuclear suicide, will be the greatest the world has ever known. Our country and industry will continue to grow at a truly marvelous rate, but with a wonderful outlook like this, it's not the time to drag your feet. On the contrary, it's the perfect, the ideal time for building the foundation for the kind of future you want for yourself and your family. It's the time to become outstanding in your particular specialty and grow along with a dynamic economy.

But here's the paradox, it is historically true that during good times the reverse occurs. It is under the fair skies of a healthy economy that you'll find the greatest amount of complacency and the least amount of effort. We all know that the time to harvest the hay is when the sun is shining, but it's really amazing how small the percentage who does that.

Challenging Decision

Becoming an entrepreneur or being self-employed is a challenging decision to make. It takes competence and strategic thinking to be in charge of your own economy.

Would you call yourself a creative person? Let's look at the characteristics of creative people. A study of leaders shows certain traits are always apparent in the creative person. Perhaps no person has them all, but those such as Edison, Kettering, Bell, Einstein, Shakespeare, and the modern creative persons including Musk, Gates, Bezos, and Zuckerberg certainly have many of the following twenty-four characteristics:

1. **Drive,** the desire to work hard and long.

2. **Courage,** tenacity of purpose.

3. **Goals.** Creative people know what they want and go after goals with vigor.

4. **Knowledge.** They have an insatiable thirst for knowledge. They know the subject, do the homework, constantly study it, and vigorously seek total knowledge of the subject area.

5. **Good health.** Creative people keep physically fit.

6. **Optimism.** The creative person is usually optimistic and positive, believes in people, tries hard to be part of the solution to a problem—not part of the problem.

7. **Enthusiasm.** Creative people are enthusiastic, have a zest for life, lives fully.

8. **Honesty.** This person is frank, forthright, honorable, has integrity, and is above all, intellectually honest.

9. **Good judgment.** Creative people have good judgment, searches for facts, evaluates them, tries to always understand first, then judges.

10. **Chance-taker.** They don't fear failure. Creative people know failure is often a stepping stone to success.

11. **Enterprising.** The creative person courageously takes on jobs others don't want or jobs others have failed to accomplish. They are daring and bold and don't try the impossible or ridiculous; not afraid to try the unknown. An opportunity seeker.

12. **Outgoing.** Creative people make friends easily, encourages people and ideas to grow in their presence.

13. **Dynamic.** Energetic, on the move.

14. **Persuasive.** Knows how to sell.

Success comes from ideas.

15. **Articulate.** They have verbal skill and competence, uses active verbs and simple words to communicate.

16. **Patient.** Creative people are patient with others, impatient with self.

17. **Perfectionist.** A creative person is always striving for excellence and will not tolerate mediocrity particularly in self.

18. **Sensitive.** These people's minds are always open and highly tuned to life around them.

19. **Flexible.** They are pliable and resilient, not rigid in their thinking.

20. **Sense of humor.** Creative people laugh easily and enjoy a good story.

21. **Curious and inquisitive.** A creative person is forever asking, "Why?"

22. **Versatile.** Creative people do many things well.

23. **Individualistic.** Nonconforming, aggressive, fearless.

24. **Creative.** Creative people know how to imagine, how to put combinations together and think in new terms. They think first, and then judge thoughts afterward.

That's the creative person.

How did you score as a creative person? Twenty-four out of twenty-four? That's pretty good! That makes you about one in a million. You'll go far!

In truth, we're all creative creatures. Each of us has been given unique gifts; and it has been written that to those who are given much, they must be willing to give much. But what comes first, receiving or giving?

As we enter the workforce, take on a new job or career, or go into a negotiation, there's always that tendency to ask, "What's in it for me?" What happens when a creative, competent person reverses that strategy and enters a relationship by thinking, "What can I do for you," or, "What's in it for you?"

Creative Careers

Advertising is perhaps one of the most creative careers—in fact, in my opinion, the most wonderful development of the modern commercial age. It is the maker or breaker of business, big or little. It is the one factor of successful sales that is most apt to be overlooked by the merchants and businesspeople of small towns and cities. Advertising is the power that will make a small success grow into a larger success. It is a science that requires study and character. Advertising cannot succeed if based on untruth. It must be built on faith and integrity.

As I've traveled around the country, every time I see a place of business, no matter how large or small, a quaint restaurant, local service station, big grocery store, or a large industrial plant, I try to think of ways in which better advertising could substantially improve the public's opinion of the business with a resulting increase in sales. And where there are more sales, there are more jobs.

A person in business for any length of time tends to take his or her place for granted along with the products that are sold, and frequently don't keep either up to snuff. Every business person should determine what kind of image is represented in the eyes of the customers and prospects and keep that image clean, neat, friendly, and attractive. They should think of new and better ways to advertise their business and make certain the business is worth advertising.

One thing is certain, far too many small business people feel that the way to succeed is to spend as little money as possible and try to make as large a profit as possible. This is the quickest way on earth to business suicide.

I knew a man out West who was strategic thinker who made an extremely profitable career out of buying small family businesses that were failing and selling them for large profits to new buyers. His method was uniformly simple. Usually, the business was advertised for sale. The family operating the business, let's say it was a restaurant, was anxious to sell before they lost any more money and would sell at quite a sacrifice just to unload the business. By paying cash, the man could really drive a bargain.

As soon as the thankful former owners had departed, my friend went to work creatively renovating the business. He personally supervised a complete refurbishing, and when he was through, it was modern, attractive, and clean. He then hired new help, personally trained them in good customer relations, and personally managed the facelifted business with excellent advertising and personal, cheerful attention to customers. The old, dirty

Advertising requires study and character built on faith and integrity.

mimeograph menus were gone along with everything else that stamped the place as being on its last legs.

Soon the business would be thriving. The service was terrific, the food excellent, and the personal attention by the new owner to every detail soon had the business earning an excellent profit. He would then sell the business at its new value, which netted him a really substantial profit. He'd usually follow this with a long vacation and then come back and repeat the process in another part of town.

He knew there was nothing wrong with the restaurant business or any of the other businesses he bought and sold. It was just a matter of solving problems by thinking through each circumstance with mental clarity and creativity.

Too many people think that all they have to do is own a business, and start counting the money. Business doesn't work that way.

A point worth remembering is that there are no good or bad businesses. Good management can turn a failing business into a success just as bad management can ruin the most successful business. So if you're considering buying a business, don't ask, "Is this a good business?" just take the time to thoroughly examine the place, inside and outside, and you can tell a lot about the management.

One Good Imaginative Idea

An interesting true story appeared in the magazine, *The American Salesman,* and I'd like to pass it along to you. It shows you the value of one good idea and what it can be worth.

One day, an efficiency expert named Ivy Lee was interviewing Charles Schwab, president of Bethlehem Steel company. Lee outlined his organization's service to Schwab and ended by saying, "With our service, you'll know how to manage better."

To which Schwab replied, "I'm not managing as well now as I know how to. What we need is not more knowing, but more doing. Not knowledge, but action. If you can give us something to pep us up to do the things we already know we ought to do, I'll gladly listen to you and pay you anything within reason you ask."

"Fine," answered Lee, "I can give you something in 20 minutes that'll step up your action, in doing, at least 50 percent."

Schwab was interested, so Lee handed Schwab a blank note sheet from his pocket and said, "Write on this paper the six most important tasks you have to do tomorrow." That took about three minutes. "Now number them in order of their importance," he said, that took about five minutes.

Then Lee said, "Now put this paper in your pocket, and the first thing tomorrow morning, look at item one and start working on it until it's finished. Then tackle number two in the same way. Then item three and so on, do this until quitting time. Don't be concerned if you've only finished one or two, you'll be working on the most important ones. The others can wait. If you can't finish them all by this method, you couldn't have with any other method either. And without some system, you'd probably not even have decided which was the most important. Do this every working day. After you've convinced yourself of the value of this system, have your men try it. Try it as long as you wish, and then send me a check for what you think it was worth."

The whole interview between Lee and Schwab lasted about 20 or 30 minutes. In a few weeks, Schwab sent Lee a check for $25,000 with a letter saying the lesson was the most profitable from a money standpoint that he had ever learned.

"In five years using this plan, it was largely responsible," Lee claimed, "for turning the, at that time, unknown Bethlehem Steel company into the biggest independent steel producer in the world. And it helped to make Charlie Schwab a hundred-million dollars and the best known steelman in the world."

That's the story of the man who made $25,000 in about 30 minutes with a single great idea, and that was

Solving problems involves thinking through each circumstance with mental clarity and creativity.

in the days when $25,000 was a fortune—and you could keep all of it.

Of course, the reason I've told you the story is twofold:

One, since it worked so well for Charles Schwab, you might want to try the same thing yourself. You'll be pleasantly surprised at the number of things you will accomplish, and in far less time, simply by tackling them one at a time and in the order of their importance.

And two, it goes a long way to show the value of an idea, an idea for improving a given situation. Ideas are, always have been and always will be, the most valuable things on earth. As Winston Churchill said, "No idea is so outlandish that it should not be considered."

Your Boss, the Customer

I want to tell you a little story which could make a wonderful difference in your life. You may already know about everything I'm going to say. If you do, you're a remarkable person and according to the latest statistics, you belong to the top 5 percent of all the working people in the world. You ought to be congratulated.

If you don't know about what I'm going to say, you've been holding yourself back not only on the job, but you're also missing a big percentage of the greatest joy in life. I want to talk about your relationship with your boss. How you handle this relationship will determine your success or failure. It will determine how much money you make or do not make, and it will determine whether you're a happy person or an unhappy person. So, let's talk about you and your boss.

Who is your boss? You have only one, and every working person from the president of the largest corporation to the shoe-shiner has the same boss. Your boss is simply the customer. There never has been, there is not now, and there never will be any boss but the customer. You customer is the one boss you must please. Everything you own, the customer has paid for. The customer buys your home, your cars, your clothes—pays for your vacations and puts your children through school. Your customer pays your doctor bills and writes every paycheck you will ever receive—and gives you every promotion you will ever obtain during your lifetime. And your customer will discharge you if you are displeasing.

Sometimes, particularly these days of seemingly complex economics and big business, we lose sight of just what business is. Our money is the result of our production that is traded for what we need and want, and it's here that logical discrimination comes into the picture.

Since our money is the result of our work, it's left to our discretion as to where we spend it. Here is where the customer assumes the role of boss. Customers will spend their money only with those whom they feel have earned it, and this is as it should be.

You and I are exactly the same way. If someone treats you badly in any way, you instinctively feel that the person has not earned your business, and you will withhold it. Over a period of time, this amounts to a really substantial penalty. This amount of money can be lost by not realizing who the boss really is. The same thing applies to our clothes, drug items, hardware, cleaning, gasoline, automobiles, everything we purchase. This money pays your salary and mine if we earn it. And our prosperity as individuals hinges directly on our attitude toward what we do for a living.

For example, the man who works on an automotive assembly line might not think much about the car at the point of sale, nor about the family that will eventually buy and travel in that car. But that family pays his salary, and they will withhold the purchase of the car he works on if it does not earn their respect and admiration. If you doubt this even for a moment, think of the cars that were once popular, yet are no longer on the road. This applies to all products.

Success Is Earned

Day by Day

Having earned a successful place in the economy should not be confused with keeping it. It must be earned every day, year in, year out. There's not a company that could not go out of business. Everything depends on how the boss is treated, the boss being the customer, and yet the customer is eminently fair just as you are. If the customer is treated with the importance deserved, your boss can in a few years bring a lot of other people into your place of business.

Now let me tell you something you may not have thought about. If you got in your car and started driving across the country, you'd pass many thousands of businesses from small restaurants, drug stores, grocery stores, gas stations to great sprawling corporate

Your prosperity hinges directly on your attitude toward what you do for a living.

complexes, covering hundreds of acres and employing thousands of people. By simply looking at each one, you can tell how they're treating the boss—the customer.

Always remember that your rewards are an exact proportion to your service. That's right. We're paid exactly what we earn, but no more. And you can tell by looking at any business exactly what it has earned by seeing what it has. It's the same with people. We get back exactly what we earn and not a penny more. And this again is just the way it should be.

Scales of Life

A person might be underpaid for a while, but the scales of life must balance eventually, and we will in the end receive just what we've earned. There are of course two ways we're paid for what we do. One is *tangible* in the form of money and the other is *intangible,* but just as important. To many, the intangible is more important. This latter form of payment comes in the form of inner satisfaction, in the form of joy as a result of accomplishment.

It also comes in the form of satisfaction in position and the standing it gives us. So each of us is paid in these two ways, money and satisfaction, and there's a very simple way to increase both of these forms of income. You may wonder how I can say that I can tell you of a simple way to increase your income from the standpoint of money as well as inner satisfaction. Yet I can and you'll be able to see and spend the results.

First, *I want you to understand and believe completely the great law that lies as the foundation of all life, business and personal—our rewards in life will be in exact proportion to our service.* The more you think about this and observe people and businesses in their true light, the more you will see the undeniable truth of it.

Now, try as best you can to estimate the proportion of your total ability you have been giving to your work. I don't think anyone gives 100 percent. I don't think it's possible to give 100 percent day in and day out. I know I don't. But estimate what you consider to be the percentage of 100 percent you have been giving to your work. Would you say it's been 30 percent, 50 percent? Try to decide.

Since your rewards will be in exact proportion to your service, you can increase your income both financially and from an inner satisfaction standpoint simply by narrowing the distance between what you have been giving to your work and the 100 percent you could give under ideal conditions. You don't have to ask for a raise. The income will appear of its own accord and in the right time. You may want to question this fact of life, but try to take my word for it.

The second point *I want to make is that if you begin to do your work better, better than you've ever done before, you will immediately begin to receive incalculably more inner satisfaction.* You'll also find that what may have been a boring or uninteresting job will take on new meaning and interest. No matter what it is you do during the entire working day, try in every case to do a little more than you have to, more than you're being paid for, because unless you do more than you're being paid for now, you can't hope for or justify an increase in pay.

The third point *I want to make is that each of us is interdependent.* As pointed out earlier, other people pay our salaries, buy our homes, clothes, feed, and educate our children. Therefore, we depend upon others for our very lives just as they must depend upon us. If we expect others to give us excellent service and find products for the money we spend, doesn't it make good sense that we should treat them the same way? Every hour spent at our work should be spent in the attempt to give the best of which we're capable, a baker's dozen for the money our company's customers spend for our products and services and with which our salaries are paid.

A person who tries to get the maximum return for the minimum of effort is only kidding himself. This kind of individual actually shrinks as a person, as a human being, and he has no real place in a dynamic and swiftly changing world. Sooner or later, the scales will balance. They must, for that is the law whether we like it or not.

The fourth point *is to try each day to find some way the work you're doing can be improved.* Here again, you're guaranteeing an increase in your income in both categories. We all know the cynical type of individual who laugh

Spend every hour at your work attempting to give the best of what you're capable of giving.

at this. I know them, you know them, but I don't know one who can be said to be doing well, do you? I know lots of men and women who are at the top of their fields who live their lives every day in the way I have suggested in these four points.

Rather than go along with someone who's never proved in his own life that he knows what he's talking about, I'd prefer to believe the one who said, "As you sow, so shall he reap." I'm sure you would rather follow the advice of a successful person who is more qualified to speak than the know-it-all who's behind in his installment payments. Anyway, it's worth a test.

Four Simple Suggestions

If you follow my suggestions for the next year, you will definitely be a different person living a rich, rewarding, and meaningful life. These four suggestions are simple but life-changing:

1. Remember that your rewards in life will be in exact proportion to your service.

2. By giving your work a larger percentage of your capabilities and talents, you will increase your income substantially.

3. Since your life depends on others, treat others in every facet of your life exactly as

you want others to treat you. If you expect others to give you excellent products and services for the money you and your family spend, then you should make certain that your job is handled as excellently as possible, since other people's money pays your salary.

4. Try to find some way every day your work can be improved—and above all, know your boss, the customer.

Treat your boss, your customer, with respect, care, courtesy, and good humor deserved. Remember, your customer pays all of your bills every month and will buy everything you will ever own. Your boss may be coarse, crude, ignorant, selfish, conniving, and a savage, and often will be. When so, it is more important than ever that you treat your customer with all the care and attention you can muster.

But most people are nice people. They're people like you and me who want to be liked, who want to get along, who want to be friends. They have problems and sorrows of their own about which we're not aware, and they have bad days and disappointments. Make sure that the time they are with you is a high point in their day and that they want to come back not just because of your company— but because of you.

If you make these four suggestions part of your daily life for a year, you will be surprised and delighted, and you'll find you don't want to live any other way. If you're already living this way, you know what I mean.

JOURNAL

IMAGINING CREATIVELY

In what ways are you a strategic thinker?

_____

_____

_____

_____

_____

_____

_____

_____

_____

_____

_____

_____

_____

_____

_____

_____

_____

What are some ways you can improve
your creativity in your daily process?

_____
_____
_____
_____
_____
_____
_____
_____
_____
_____
_____
_____
_____
_____
_____
_____
_____
_____

*What are objects or views around you
right now that you could let your mind
focus on and uncover ideas and details
you have not thought of before?*

_____

_____

_____

_____

_____

_____

_____

_____

_____

_____

_____

_____

_____

_____

_____

_____

_____

_____

Try looking at something now and seeing it in a different way. Write down what comes to mind.

CONCLUSION

YOUR GOOD IDEAS

I want you to imagine a mental picture of a gold mine or an oil field before it was discovered, no busy noisy machinery, no crowds of workers moving around, no trucks and heavy equipment, just land covered with prairie grass and stretching as far as your eye can see to the distant horizon.

Now, under that peaceful and innocent-looking piece of prairie is a wide deep lake of oil or a mother lode of gold worth millions. But you'd never know it was there, would you? Before these discoveries were made, thousands of people must have rode and walked right over them without realizing that right under their feet was a king's ransom in riches beyond their wildest dreams.

Someone had to come along looking for it and willing to risk digging for it, right? Someone had to suspect it was there and start looking, and the chances of hitting pay dirt with the first shovelful were pretty slim, but someone knew if he kept looking and kept digging, he'd find it.

Well, you and I and everyone else have free title to the richest continent on earth. It's called the human mind and it has produced just about everything you see and hear around you. It comes as standard equipment at birth and maybe that's why most of us never use it. Our mind came free and we've come to the point when we don't value things that are free anymore.

The greatest thing on earth is a good idea—which comes about by strategic thinking with mental clarity, solving problems, and being creative. Take the person who got the idea to dig under that prairie grass.

Your idea is the cause...resulting in good fortune.

Discovering a fortune was only the result. His idea to dig was the cause and it was his idea that resulted in millions for him.

Now consider: how many ideas can you come up with in one single day? Twenty days? Thirty days?

Let's say you get 20 ideas a day, that would be a hundred a week if you didn't think on weekends. That would be 5,200 ideas a year, 5,200 holes you would be drilling on the world's richest continent—your own mind.

Remember, one great idea can make you rich. All you need is one good idea that can be your gold mine, your oil well. If you know anything about the law of averages, you realize that before long you will have the idea you've been looking for. Just because the first ten or one hundred aren't any good, don't give up. The more dry holes, the closer you are to what you're looking for, your big idea, the one that will change your life.

The best way to prospect your mind is to get up an hour earlier in the morning and write down twenty ideas for improving what you now do for a living. The chances are that right now, as Russell Conwell said, "Right now you are standing right in the middle of your own acre of diamonds. What you're looking for is the idea that's bigger than you are and that will keep you challenged and interested for a long time to come."

Some stories are so good they never grow old, and one of them is called Acres of Diamonds. No one knows

Fields of gold and acres of diamonds are the wild imaginations and opportunities all around us.

who told it the first time. It's supposed to be true, and of course it is, in that it's happened thousands of times to thousands of people in thousands of different situations.

But the man who made the story famous in this country at least, was Dr. Russell H. Conwell, who lived from 1843 to 1925 and who, by telling the story from one end of the world to the other, raised $6 million with which he founded Temple University in Philadelphia and thus fulfilled his dream to build a really fine school for poor but deserving young men.

Dr. Conwell told the story, Acres of Diamonds, more than 6,000 times and attracted great audiences wherever he appeared. You may be as familiar with the story as I am, but it isn't the story that's so important in itself— and you're probably wondering if I'll ever get around to telling it.

Well, yes, I will, but the important thing is that we *apply the principle of the story to our lives.*

The story is about a farmer who lived in Africa at the time diamonds were discovered there. When a visitor to his farm told him of the millions being made by men who were discovering diamond mines, the farmer promptly sold his farm and left to search for diamonds himself. He wandered all over the continent yet found no diamonds. And as the story goes, he finally penniless, in poor health and despondent, threw himself into a river and drowned.

Long before this, the man who had bought the farm from the farmer found a large unusual-looking stone in the creek bed that ran through the farm. He took it home and put it on his mantle as a curio. Enter here, the same visitor who had told the original farmer about the diamond discoveries. This man examined the stone and then told the new owner that he had discovered one of the largest diamonds ever found and that it was worth a king's ransom.

To his surprise, the new farmer told the man the entire farm was covered with stones of that kind. And to make a long story short, if it isn't already too late, the farm, which the first farmer had sold so that he could go look for diamonds, turned out to be one of the richest diamond mines in the world.

The point Dr. Conwell made was that the first farmer had owned acres of diamonds but had made the mistake of not examining what he had before he ran off to something he hoped would prove to be better. He would then point out that each of us is like that first farmer. No matter where we live or what we do, we are surrounded by acres of diamonds if we will simply look for them.

Like the curious-appearing stones that covered the farm, your opportunities might not appear to be diamonds at first glance, but a little study, a deeper examination and some polishing will reveal our opportunities for what they really are.

Each person—you included—has deep reservoirs of ability that we habitually fail to use simply because we fail to think strategically to develop ourselves to our true stature—and there is lurking in our daily work as well as in ourselves, acres of diamonds.

ABOUT EARL NIGHTINGALE

Earl Nightingale (1921-1989) was a man of many talents and interests—nationally syndicated radio personality, entrepreneur, philosopher, US Marine, and more. One thread united all his pursuits—a passion for excellence and living a meaningful existence.

Earl Nightingale's life began simply. He grew up in Long Beach, California. His parents had little money, and his father disappeared when he was 12. But even as a boy, Earl was always asking questions, always reading books in the local public library, wanting to understand the way life works.

Stationed aboard the battleship USS Arizona, Earl Nightingale was one of a handful of survivors when that ship was destroyed and sank at Pearl Harbor. After being separated from the Marine Corps and starting with practically nothing, over the next ten years he founded and headed four corporations. In addition, he wrote, sold, and produced fifteen radio and television programs per week.

Nightingale appeared on all major radio networks. For four years he was the star of the dramatic series *Sky King,* which was carried on more than 500 stations of the Mutual Radio Network. He also began an insurance agency, and in twelve months led it from last to sixth place in the nation with one of the world's largest companies.

The Nation's Press carried the astounding story of the phenomenally successful young man who, at age 35, had become financially independent. He produced his famous recording of *The Strangest Secret,* revealing how anyone can make the most of his or her own capabilities and can attain a rich full measure of success and happiness, right in his or her present job or position. Its theme: "How to achieve greater success and enjoy greater happiness and peace of mind."

At the time, this inspiring recording broke sales records, selling in the multimillions to major industries, retailers and salespeople, clubs and associations, parents, students, and people in virtually all walks of life. His masterful recording has been adapted into books and videos.

THANK YOU FOR READING THIS BOOK!

If you found any of the information helpful, please take a few minutes and leave a review on the bookselling platform of your choice.

BONUS GIFT!

Don't forget to sign up to try our newsletter and grab your free personal development ebook here:

soundwisdom.com/classics

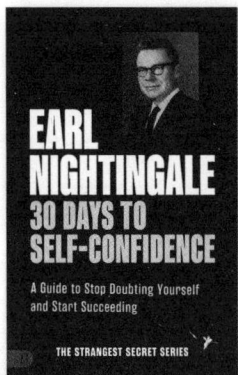

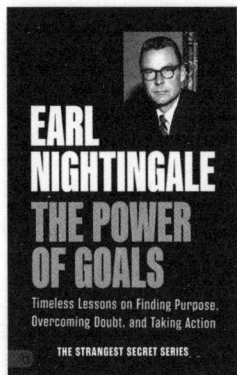

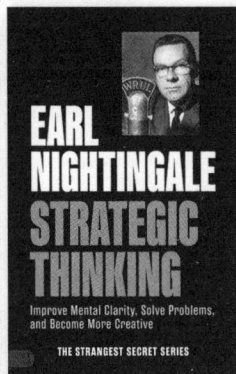